Copyright © 2023 Natasha Soares All rights reserved

Copyright notice: All rights reserved under the International Copyright Conventions. No part of this book may be reproduced or transmitted in any form or by any means, electronic or mechanical including photocopying and recording, or by any information storage and retrieval system without prior written permission of the publisher, except in the case of brief quotations embodied in reviews and certain other non-commercial uses permitted by copyright law.

TORONTO • 2023

BEYOND THE HEART'S VEIL

THE ANTHOLOGY
OF A
SOUL'S ASCENSION

NATASHA SOARES

TORONTO • 2023

This book is dedicated to:

My sweet earth angels, Macio and Sienna. Thank you for choosing me.
My other half, Bruno. I can't imagine going through life without you by my side.

Dreams are born from saying hello.

I am so glad you are here.

Within these pages, you will find a piece of my heart that has been nourished by the written word.

I hope that one of my poems resonates with you, or at the very least, will ignite your curiosity. Above all, I am eternally grateful for your time and support.

Thank you a million times over.

Oceans of gratitude,

Natasha Soares

This Diary belongs to

Natasha

CONTENTS

BEGINNING

Page i. Beginning
Page ii. Forward

YEARNING

Page 2. Lunacy Of Sleep
Page 3. Infusion
Page 4. The Beating Ring
Page 5. The Road Runs Out
Page 6. Close To You
Page 7. Remnants Of The Past
Page 8. Making Colours
Page 9. Grasping
Page 10. Velvet Artisan

ESCAPISM

Page 12. He Sat In Sun-Kissed Masses
Page 13. Implore Him
Page 14. In A Field By 9th Line
Page 15. Unearthly Creatures
Page 16. Wine Virgin

MELANCHOLY

Page 18. Three Words
Page 19. Lost Vigil Of Love
Page 20. Seething
Page 21. Desperately Devoted
Page 22. Cold Cotton
Page 23. Sing A Song Of Blue
Page 24. You Cannot Choose Love
Page 25. I Cannot Love You Until
Page 26. Her Hearts Castle Fell
Page 27. On My Way Home

CONTENTS

SUBLIME

Page 29. May's Endeavour
Page 30. My King
Page 31. Sweet Slumber
Page 32. Faultless Vanish
Page 33. Plucked Carnation

SOFT HEART

Page 35. Two Methods
Page 36. My Only Sister
Page 38. He Is My Sweet Tooth
Page 40. Wed My Dream
Page 41. From A Distance

OBLIVION

Page 43. City Of Peace
Page 44. Unordinary Whimper
Page 45. Astral
Page 46. Iridescent Mystic
Page 47. Debonair
Page 48. Gladiatrix
Page 49. Silver Thread

CONTENTS

ETERNAL

Page 51. The Garden Of His Face
Page 52. Summer Peach
Page 53. Unhinged
Page 54. Mirror Moments
Page 55. Prince
Page 56. Summer Dream
Page 57. Spiritual Laceration
Page 58. Mid-Day Vibrato
Page 59. I Owe You An Apology

LETTERS

Page 61. Running For The Thrill
Page 62. Assert
Page 63. Forever Bond
Page 64. Ex Nihilo
Page 65. Deposits
Page 66. Old Lady Love
Page 67. Release
Page 68. Motherly Hues
Page 69. Death
Page 70. Hungry Soul
Page 71. Heartache

FINAL ACT

Page 73. Thank You

"Having a soft heart in a cruel world takes courage, not weakness."

Katherine Henson

LUNACY OF SLEEP

Sleep can be a dangerous thing
in not knowing if what happened was a dream
or an actual stir within your heart.

INFUSION

Infuse, delight, in the purest form,
even in the remnants of your dreams.
Or be condemned to a life of hiatus,
and uninspired muses.
Let pinpricks dictate your syllables,
the blood is your lyricist.

THE BEATING RING

I swear it, thought I heard the telephone ring.
The sweet jing-a-ling.

Neither or, it was just
the thumping of my impatient heart.

THE ROAD RUNS OUT

Before the bricks cease on this road I roam,
Oh, the sights I yearn to see, the places to comb,
The Amazon's river, rushing and wide,
Treetops swaying, kissed by the breeze's stride.

Before my last breath, my heart's final beat,
I seek forgiveness, a prayer I entreat,
Universe, forgive the sins that within me reside,
As I face the end with my breaths aside.

Frail hands, weathered and old, receive divine grace,
Blessings bestowed upon me in love's embrace,
For the wondrous love I have known and felt,
From the heavens above, where my soul's dwelt.

Time, oh time, it raced too fast, too fleet,
Unveiling a cruel deadline I'm forced to meet,
My appointment has come, bidding me fly,
Now, alas, it's time to bid my good-bye.

CLOSE TO YOU

Hold this poem in your pocket, wallet, or purse.
Perhaps tack it on your wall.

Never forget I am here for you.
Thick and thin, through it all.

REMNANTS OF THE PAST

Always remember
There is no time like the past.
There are no memories better.
You and I are young and wild
Living the dream together.

There is no friend like an old friend
Who has shared our morning days.
There is no greeting like her welcome
No other kind words than her praise.

MAKING COLOURS

Who else could make the colours of the aurora borealis rise off my skin where he strokes my forearm?

Or send needles of ice tinkling blue through my brain when he looks into my eyes?

Love changes everything.

I drink every kiss down to its end and yet, my mouth still aches like a dry cave.

GRASPING

He said to me "I'll buy you the world."
Quick kiss and stare.
Presents to ones heart's desire, he dared not care.

And he said to me "Whatever you want, you got."
But face-up palms.
Left me grasping at air.

VELVET ARTISAN

Moist stars wet with light, immortalized against a velvety cape,
She cried beneath the moon's soft glow while her secrets took shape.

With every tale she weaves, a piece of her soul take flight,
In the vastness of her mind, a constellation of light.

And when she cries beneath the moon's embrace,
Her tears, like ink, give birth to new grace.

A languorous release amid the satin of night,
Her heart finds its call, a writer's passion, a timeless scrawl.

"Que sera, sera. Whatever will be, will be."

Doris Day

HE SAT IN SUNKISSED MASSES

He sat in the sun kissed masses,
reminiscent of a beautiful contemporary scene-shaping gem.

A revered blend of flesh flashing visuals,
an exterior of a shaking soul.

Deepest beats came from his heart,
heaviest baseline grooves I ever heard.

The flow that sits instant on the ear,
silenced not by a frenzied crowd.

He all the while, immersed me with his sublime breezy gush,
without airs of his sultry urbanized glossy power.

IMPLORE HIM

Best be known, was there a caterwaul of a man,
Bucolic cry heard by my inglenook, crestfallen on flames.

Doleful, perhaps somnolent under a pale moonstruck sheet sleeping,
briny deep wafts of pungent dishwater and cheap canned heat.

Harrowing singleton who sits asunder nightlong,
splintered bones and sputtered joy, half-past swart falter.

Thy broached dulcet soul agleam,
I wonder sweet, sugary.

Frozen pearly grey cobble stones his bassinet,
chill deep of winters palm.

I beseech, be saint his silhouette,
to oust his torrent dreams.

Isle of tears I've bemoaned,
in tune with he.

Join me fortune-less soul, among emotional warmth,
belong in earth-slight by the whole of the countless hearts that burn.

IN A FIELD BY 9TH LINE

He poured bitter lemon, topped with malted milk,
gingerly handed me a fever few chosen new still dew-scented.

Weathered yellow wicker seating that scored designs,
avant-garde blueprint formed whilst sitting from dawn to dusk
underneath his coconut palm.

Inexperienced clover plucked to mark a page green,
mosey warble fly jazzed nearby until finally landing on his Bermuda
short thigh.

Mumble speak like his tongue was toffee,
coatings and sauces he covered his words lightly,
spoke softly when picking the pits from plums.

We wasted so many days smelling of earth after rain,
itching bites that were soothed by evening wafts
as he left deep-seated imprints on nearby blades of grass.

UNEARTHLY CREATURES

Senseless beauty enraptured
between the bluish curtains of nightfall's shimmer.
They found themselves, uneasily settled in the desert of gambling fears.

Bête noir's sunlit vapours wheezed sprightliness into their windowless eyes.
Ribcages exhaled the exhumed sighs,
myriads of May's ethereal cull.

Oh vigour of the fresh, dearest of the sweets.
Predestined en masse,
throughout the polished sleepless thrust.

They met among rustic woven metal,
slung beneath a resplendent cascade of waterfalls.
Ringing peal throughout the echo halls of magnificent lights.

Land of the victimless brought their paths to the oasis of assassins.
Where their unmoral tangibility of youth and amour,
buttoned up among days and nights in sin.

The mountains sneer in neon signs, wide valleys of a temporal city
camouflaging their craze.
Bottled in legions of memories in a city they made theirs.

WINE VIRGIN

Fed wine gum to my only one.
Yearlings till midsummer's eventide.
White grapes blazon from one end,
On the waxen table spread, twittered the whiter shade.

Bud-break at first blush amid the morning breeze.
Thoughts bursting into blooming dispositions.
Nature's most natural blends fancy-free,
Quartz of ripe vino, not rotted, for his inamorata star

"As above, so below."

Hermes Trismegistus

THREE WORDS

Three words loosely strung together
To form a sentence true
All I feel inside
Is that of

I
    miss
            you.

LOST VIGIL OF LOVE

...beckoning every fortnight, wailing formidable truths against summer's wind tongues.
Timidly rapping on the rusty traps of muted ears.
I sit upon hours of anguished plagues;
my most woebegone nights were vigils of what would be love.

...kisses that outnumber reasoned words.
Trumpeting abiding love and alluding to amity.
The circumference of all things and the center of all joy.
It is not fingertips that trace teardrop scores upon the back, the circumference of all things and the center of love.

...memories sing tuneless lullabies where we were united first, in the dwelling that sheltered our love.
Afterward, in the hearts that burned with it.
Remember this bosom held a ferocious exteriority that shelved my amore away from his fragrant balm of syrupy clemency.
The inexperience of rapturous love artlessly compelled even more in the pursuit of its anguish.

...his hands drew and regretfully languished and outlined unity that first sought dwelling in the unspeakable truth of our melody.
He hearkened the speechless smirk of wanting nothing.
Nothing of yours,
Yet all of you.

SEETHING

It was the kind of hurt that dulled your vision and singed your lashes with every blink.
It scorched my cheekbones and with pain like that, I'd rather sleep.

That kind of festering that others could see in the pupil in a moments grace. Or hear it on the phone a million miles away.

It manifested itself in my walk, shoulders weighted and in deep-seated steps. Slowly and barely, I'd rather not walk at all, but I do dare.

You'd smell it in my sheets, pillows warm and damp.
Satin pillows with tear dropped stains.

It's the pain that removes the sheen from my hair, matted to the bowed crown. Kleenex strewed room amongst slippers & curtains drawn.

Purified despair.

DESPERATELY DEVOTED

In depths of love, he carries the weight,
Enduring immense feelings, never abate.
I watch him nuzzle, seek a smile,
A dance of forgetfulness, for a while.

Spoon-feeding, speaking like a child,
Yearning for a connection, tender and mild.
The radio's tunes, a touch of home,
All to help her stay, not to roam.

One-way conversations, unanswered queries,
Missing words like "son" and "I love you" dearly.
Casual banter, now replaced by silence,
Uncertainty, sorrow, his heart's defiance.

Can she grasp his love, its depth and might,
In her lost thoughts, a flicker of light?
Could she fathom the pain of his near-far,
As his tears pale to his lonely memoir?

Dignity stolen, bit by bit,
He strives to mend, refusing to quit.
Her thoughts and words, scattered and torn,
He tries to assemble, forlorn.

He fights to bring her back, to remember,
Whispering "mommy," seeking her laughter.
But despair fills his eyes, when she's far astray,
On a path he cannot follow, come what may.

COLD COTTON

Your scent has left my pillow.
I search to find a lingering trace.
Knowing it has fled, as you with my heart.
Leaves a bed an even sadder place.

SING A SONG OF BLUE

My baby, he left me
To decipher the colour
Dark blue.

And even though I never
Sang the shade
I sung.

My baby, he left me to bury his feelings
Where they could not be found
He dug.

And even though I swore I'd never
I wrung my hands in despair
I sought.

Cooked and cultivated rich
In a mist of cavernous pain
He wrought.

YOU CANNOT CHOOSE LOVE

Darling boy, you don't choose love,
Ignoring your hearts plea is nothing...
Short of irredeemable.
Your broken heart which still beats,
Screams in infuriating pain...
Oh darling boy, you don't choose love.
Cracking bones give and bend,
But thumbscrews cannot loosen...
A lover's tryst.
Darling boy, you don't choose love,
Never let smoke invade your eyes...
Because of others.
Oh darling boy, you don't choose love,
Elixir of bright colors and streaming truths...
They find you.

I CANNOT LOVE YOU UNTIL

These words he spoke were those of a fable;
Heart fisted and adorned with angst.
Spewed from a mouth that once uttered with a honeyed tongue;
Reigned someone new that calloused almost at once.

His words were like fire I warmed my hands too;
Somber orange blossoms mixed with hospital smells and sounds of gnashing of teeth.
A disease retched and tore through, sweet girl don't cry;
Soothsayers could say their carriage knowingly of better times.

Yet
All I ever wanted, I never had;
Was for him to love me, but I amble among the fruitless.
I beseech among the beggars;
And pleaded and toiled among the sinners.

Hopelessly I cried,
Desperately I slept.
Imperfectly I doubted,
Sorrowfully I tried.

In aim for, and of that benevolence he had to keep at bay.
Nail scratching at what-ifs, bleeding fingers grasp at the magnetism of his being;
Pulling at those strong hands to stay and skirmish, those hands which once stroked me soundly.

Permitted to speak only through tears;
spar sweet girl, wage the war asked of you.
Golden like honey and just as sweet; forsaken words
of a discarded deed.

HER HEARTS CASTLE FELL

Burning tears as
firebrands
across my cheek.
Drops on buds to future blossom
encumbered fields
of peccadillo.

Seething scorned
by enriched delight
upon my poor, poor heart.
And I, by a morsel attempted to regain
decorum of the ruin
he wrought.

ON MY WAY HOME

I'm frail but young
My neck seems to bare the load
A suitcase full of lonely thoughts
That no one cares to know.

An aching back, I have
Hauls and carries with every whispered groan
Knee's knocking and shaking
Ferociously trying to carry me home.

"Worrying is like paying a debt you don't owe."

Mark Twain

MAY'S ENDEAVOUR

Sweetest love!
Daring not, but once to
Indulge in memories rapturous pain,
Blue calm evening I still languish
When love and peace do retire;
Remembering of time when the starry skies did call out your name.
Amid of the night, an innocent
fights of a heart's desire.
Drunken from deep divinest anguish, I could not sleep
A thousand and one pricks from a thorn, my tears I've poured thee;
Our love stronger by than love, of those who were older than we, I weep.
Marching time drew on, a simple, silent outstretched plea.
Never struck before by Cupids arrow that lovely May hour.
My soft verse to you, embracing my brooding kisses, that speaks gloom;
The tints that glow upon your cheeks,
Bloom like a divine flower.
Dreams of everlasting bliss.

MY KING

Oh, brooding love, tinted blood red affection;
You feed my every desire & leave me flushing at the cheeks.
Fickle, I do not know, but knowest everlasting
Lust will sustain.
Undying & contagious is your being,
I hang off your single words and wander in your tender eye.
With you, the air does not bite shrewdly and
The cold season does not draw near.
Instead I gulp the eager air and
I am sullied by your manner.
I swear by it, I profess my love.
Till then, sit my soul in a dream of passion
Call me guilty, dangerous lunacy of a fit of joy.
Come, some sweet music, give a fellowship of
Tunes to recount my admiration.
By crown, ambition, Queen with King,
I swear by it, I profess my love.

SWEET SLUMBER

As we slept,
We held hands in our sudden state of the sleeping REM.
Our hands still managed to find each other,
Underneath the confusion of twisted legs, bunched up comforters,
Covered by the blanket of the night.

FAULTLESS VANISH

Covered by the blanket of the night
Shallow breathes among the swelter
Buzzing past his reposing lips
The chum of his midnight murmurs, which
Kept my dirty eyes amongst a mirthful drift.

Betwixt crinkle-cut bedspreads and skeleton decor
Lay our robes of skin athwart Octobers unearthly glow
Stark white stars glint with a drowsy twinkle eclipse
Canary the echoes of his heavy beating heart flow.

Oh, sea of salty sad tears streaming
Dim with weeping, oh, ring the blues
Harpoon my jilted root by seizing
Crimson ribbon of hapless trues.

Gift of grief on angel winds come falling
Erstwhile, I swained his olive ashen frame
Sprightly into a wintery blush our time came calling
Unable to script our mark among the skies before it blew away.

PLUCKED CARNATION

Summer sowing borne atop upright stems,
The infinite layers of reality rendered in a clove pink floret.

Ceremonial crown linked to memories of my past Queen,
Whose days have been frequented from the blundering bumble bee.

Scalloped edge bookmark, the penchant of a fragrant childhood,
An arrangement of honeyed communication by luminary theme.

Carnation tones sit sonneting while stirring the spirit,
Through blossoms & winged favours we live by - "I love you to the sky".

"When you are not fed love on a silver spoon, you learn to lick it off knives."

Lauren Eden

TWO METHODS

In the witching time of night
When I am left without you
Pass the tedious day with sleep.
Let me forget my sorrow
And get lost in my dreams.
Or rather be destroyed by fits of insomnia
When your presence is gone.
The pillow cold and unused.
By these two comparative methods
I do some realize the poison in jest in which love
Consumes my soul.

MY ONLY SISTER

How do I capture our lives together in one poem?
Recount my admiration and love for the entire world to know
We lived down the street most of our lives
A phone call away in a moments surprise.

I remember those warm nights with our cold drinks
Our shortest dresses and even higher heels
With my dear, brown-eyed sweetheart of mine
Whom I forever asked to be my Valentine.

Through-out Europe we adventured and conquered it all
Despite our oversized luggage and empty credit cards
We'd roast all day on those white beaches so fine
Moments to remember and hold in our hearts to shine.

Over the years she's given me bracelets to cover scars
Effortlessly made me laugh at times that I cried so hard
No matter the greatest of distance in between
In those fleeting moments, sisters we will always be.

I love my love and her alone
Blessing and blest where'er she may go
I often see heaven reflected in her beautiful face
The utmost of friendships which no soul could replace.

Shows me heaven when I was blinded by hell
Knew what to say all those terrible times I fell.
She entered my heart as a protective age to guide
My sister, she continues to love me and has stayed by my side.
What through these years of ours be fleeting?
What through the years of youth be flown?
You may not be with me as much anymore
But I know you will leave me an opened door.

May we go through life always together
May there always be a "we"
Come let us kiss and gracefully part
A bright new future for us to see.

HE IS MY SWEET TOOTH

Cakes and strawberries, he is as fine.
I am so proud to call him all mine!
The crème de la crème, the icing on the cake,
Caramel popcorn and delicious frosted flakes.

I'd go as far to say that he is my mushy marshmallow,
The juiciest red and black liquorice fellow.
Cinnamon sprinkles, you are so divine
My yummy jellybean for all time.

He is the tastiest treat one could ever eat,
Donuts and cupcakes no one could beat.
Toasted tarts and fuzzy peach,
He is my popsicle on a hot afternoon beach.

If someone was to ask me, I would
tell
tell
tell

that
you
are
the

Banana to my sundae, my savoury coco bean,
That rich vanilla taste that hooked me like a fiend.

My apple sauce and warm pastry puff,
The milk to my milkshake and the warmest pie crust.
Cherry on my lips, the blueberry of my eye,
My batch of sugar cookies my fresh lemon meringue pie.
Caramel truffle, you are my cupcake too,
I don't think I could even explain how much I adore you.

Baby,
You are the yum-yum for my tum-tum
The pleasure in the dessert,
You're going to give me all the cavities,
until it really hurts.

WED MY DREAM

I'd like to marry a writer someday and live in a cramped studio apartment and listen to the rhythmic tapping of a computer keyboard at night.

I'd like to marry a painter someday and give up my body entirely as a blank canvas, awaken to new art with every brilliant sunrise.

I'd like to marry an actor someday and be taken to a red-carpet premier, adorned in diamonds as the glitz bounces off our eyes.

I'd like to marry a photographer someday, who will capture my tenaciousness and quirks behind the lens.

I'd like to marry a gardener someday so that he can tend and weed me, bud to blossom from the nectar of love. To be the dirt under his nails when he toils over me.

I'd like to marry a musician who will make music with my bones, play my hips, my ribs, my wrists, my shoulder blades. Singing me a lullaby with his delicate hands and make me moan.

I'd like to marry you someday, all the things you are and all the things you will be. And at our wedding, we will dance.

FROM A DISTANCE

He's my Prince Charming, so dashing and fine,
In armor of steel, a love so divine.
When troubles arise, he's there by my side,
Protecting and guiding, my valiant pride.

Although he will reign at a distance,
I will feel his presence near.
I keep his heart on my sleeve for resistance,
For those lonely nights that I oh-so fear.

The time when he comes is pleasing,
My blood bubbles with delight.
He keeps me sane and fights my heart from a lonesome seizing,
Every part of me he excites.

"Everything not saved will be lost."

Nintendo "Quit Screen" message

CITY OF PEACE

Dawn of 1692, as I sit in the early afternoon, just beside a dirt road, leading out of the "City of Peace" Salem.
The swaying treetops now seemed not to be the loving arms guiding me on as they use to be.
The corn that stands tall in the field, whispering sweet nothingness, left neglected.
Fruit tree's laden with fall harvest.
"Consider how torn asunder the community still is even after all these years".
No one to indulge these true words would pay heed.
The circle of the afflicted up the hill.
Naming tormentors with a misgiving heart.
What ails this town so?
Who will allay the fear back to the darkest nights?
The handing tree on Gallows hill, embraced by the sign of alliance.
I'm like the scarce mocking bird amongst others.
Throughout the town the Puritan heart turning black with hate.
Puritan righteousness gone without haste.

UNORDINARY WHIMPER

Uncut Diamonds,
she was as hard.
Shooting electricity,
she sang song of cobbled, rocky paths.
Meticulously she drank
bamboo tea.

Crossed legged, precariously, with her buttered lips,
jungle hair & wild eyes.
Lackluster & pale,
picturesque of a creature from the pages of
Baudelaire.

She as a bright eddy,
glamorous watercolors a ruin.
Inferno red, stains China rims,
scripts of ruffled mar.

Telling of hot tears,
mapping her balmy sighs…
Fans the blaze by means of
batting eyelashes black.

Sapphire views misted up,
waterproof cinematography.
While beads of sticky untruths,
rib and spar violet sparks of pain.

Calloused layers against fusty amour,
falling between the cracks of hearts custody.
It was a spectacular mess of
unadorned afflictions…

Flush before divine tea-time hour,
emerald tea sipping Queen.

ASTRAL

Beyond the realms of earthly bound,
A journey awaits for those who've found,
The path to leave the earthly plane,
And soar beyond the stars again.

With every thought and every dream,
We're given wings to make us beam,
To cast aside the chains that bind,
And find the peace we hope to find.

So let us close our earthly eyes,
And reach for skies beyond the skies,
To travel far beyond the night,
And see the beauty of the light.

And as we journey through the stars,
We'll find a world that's full of charms,
A place where love and hope abide,
And all our fear and doubts subside.

So let us journey far and wide,
And find the truth that possess inside,
And let our souls take flight once more,
To explore the astral realm and more.

IRIDESCENT MYSTIC

Crystalized intention nestled within my back pocket,
Risen from a kaleidoscope of star seed dust.

Yearning for an unordinary cosmic devotion,
Spirit wide open in a shimmering soft white glow.

Transcendent tapestry of essence rearranged,
An opal aura faceted against an ethereal burning bright.

Lifted energy with an unpolished selenite stem,
Crystal caverns of my seraphic love whispered a universal groan.

DEBONAIR

Less a woman would say she loved you always
A harem of the sacred heart.
But I only love you until Wednesday
The job half done as a lost art.

Less a woman would say she loved you always
With the week ending, I've done the best I can.
Those Wednesday afternoons are the easiest
In which I can say, you are the lesser man.

GLADIATRIX

Passionate patriot of madness,
searing crazed war.

Scarring her charcoal,
famished for more.

SILVER THREAD

We are all sewing up the seams
Of a tailor-made life.
A conscious thread passing from
The soul to physical strife.

"Enlightenment is when a wave realizes it is the ocean."

Thich Nhat Hanh

THE GARDEN OF HIS FACE

There I did see, as I glazed momentarily,
A garden in his face, which glowed brightly and almost magically.
Sweetness blossoming on his cheeks, in the softness of his pale frow.
Where the mind did sweep, and his eyes did speak a few sentences
of endured enlightenment.

Tremendous whispers of the beckoning breeze,
Caressing the ruby beauties of his heart-shaped lips.
Softer than thy petals in a morning dew mist,
His laughter echoing in which couldn't be missed.

Whose tongue does move heaven & earth,
Like the thunder clouds that bring thy mirth.
The moon does shine in his face,
That number one light, outlines and illuminates the way.

Embracing such wonders of his love undefined,
Lays triumphs and hath such wit of every kind.
To skit and contemplate, my heart fulfilled.
Viewing the garden, which was his face.

SUMMER PEACH

A difficult journey, a road fraught with pain,
A heart that yearned for a daughter, but in vain,
Yet in my womb, you grew, a precious gift from above,
A tiny life that I cherished, held close with love.

I harbored this love, kept you safe until your debut,
With each passing day, my heart grew anew,
And when you finally arrived, my sweet summer peach,
I felt complete, as if the puzzle found its missing piece.

You brought light to my life, a joy that knew no bounds,
A love so pure and true, it lifted me from the ground,
And as I held you close, my heart swelled with pride,
For you were the miracle that I had longed for, the one I had cried.

Through the difficult days, the moments of fear,
I held onto hope, knowing that you were near,
And now that you are here, my sweet little one,
I thank the stars above for giving me my summer sun.

UNHINGED

World without end, the time without light,
speaks of worry and boundless obscurity.

Camouflaged among the stars where I,
gingerly placed my unremitting heart.

No end of, no end to,
ribbons of silver vespers and pastel love whispers.

Rendered an isle of tears where antiquity danced under one's breath,
soundlessly and carelessly.

MIRROR MOMENTS

When you were a tiny soul, I cradled you tight,
In our room, I held you, inhaling your sweet light,
Admiring your features, a face so dear,
Melted by the coos, music to my ear.

In the mirror's reflection, a glimpse of us together,
I'd pause, backtrack, wanting that image to last forever,
The small you, the mother in me, embraced so tight,
In that tranquil room, our love taking flight.

Sometimes laughter bubbled, sheer luck in my core,
To cherish such moments, my heart could not ignore,
Yet tears would trickle, from joy and a knowing,
That nostalgia would touch me, its waves ever flowing.

Months passed, as I soothed you to sleep's gentle call,
In the quiet room, blinds lowered, shadows befallen,
And there, in my periphery, love's sight renews,
The image of our embrace, rekindling the fuse.

Once more, I backtrack,
Swept away by affection's glide,
In that same quiet room,
Love's tapestry untied.

PRINCE

Your sigh, like a whispered melody, softly sighs,
Under the moonlit sky, a seed of joy shall rise,
With each flutter of your dreaming eye,
Love within me intensifies, unremitting, never shy.

The subtle scent of your breath, a delicate fragrance,
Touches my heart before it reaches my senses,
Smiling, captivated by the night's romance,
How swiftly I fell, lost in your presence.

As I cradle your slumbering form against my chest,
Shoulders draped with warmth, a comforting nest,
I pass the mirror, compelled to pause, and stare,
Reflecting on the fortune in my arms, love so rare.

Those mirror moments, etched sharply in my mind,
In their calm and security, a fiery blaze I find,
Knowing not the depth of what lies ahead,
But cherishing stolen seconds, where love is spread.

Time, so fleeting, yet days sugar-coated and dear,
Until these arms no longer hold you near,
Just as my womb once cradled your being,
In memories and love, forever, we'll be fleeing.

In the depths of my being, you're entwined,
In my essence, a bond, forever aligned.
From the womb's embrace to the person you've grown,
My son, our connection, immortal, known.

From birth to womanhood, an eternal dance,
I'm an extension of you, in lifelong trance.
Endless devotion, an unbreakable tie,
Forever intertwined, as the years fly by.

SUMMER DREAM

Honey saucer eyes with pinstriped yellow hues,
Wilted maternal dreams have since left,
With the arrival of you.

Your scent plunges me into a lovesick melody,
Exalted breath, as sweet as candied milk,
Nuzzled into the nook of your neck of silk.

A lavender bouquet of your wispy fleeced hair,
Heart-shaped lips in a suckled embrace,
Holding your pacifier safe in place.

My girl, you are heaven walking on earth,
I'm blessed to see all your firsts,
Melancholy pooled in my eyes,
knowing those firsts are also final goodbyes.

SPIRITUAL LACERATION

I've held four babies in my womanly form,
From those four, two were born.

Death has lived in me without merciful respite,
From that downhearted unrooting of life.

Emotionally fraught & immortally pregnant with worry,
Ravenous pangs of loss become my story.

Tormented inertia of a soul wound,
To experience a stir within, only to suffer its adieu.

But then you both came, the dichotomy of my lost two,
Cherubim and earthbound blessings overdue.

Mother of two layered worlds & realms,
Conjoined DNA strand, a part of my existence until the end.
Dashing farewells to triumphed embraces.
Unconditionally and enduring plight of mothering stages.

MID-DAY VIBRATO

The mornings blend with the afternoons,
Bleeding, blending, alla prima.

Time is two-dimensional, conceptual, and familiar in its flow,
Reminiscent of lived moments like this and previous lives before.

On this day, the heat burrowed behind the waffling breeze,
Outside maintained the sparrows chirping like a concerto melody.

Instrumental composition paired with the sound of dishes being put away,
The laundry machine yet another note, another load for the day.

Among the first-blush symphony, my littlest scampers by my feet,
Balanced on tiny toes like a ballerina, subtle but sweet memories to keep.

Time swoops in with an invigorated tempo, sharpened by the years,
Wishing on a star for her high-pitched twitter to continue filling our days with a harmonic atmosphere.

Today like every other, sadness and happiness are in tune,
A reverberating crescendo of our best days being played and undone on this sunny day in June.

I OWE YOU AN APOLOGY

My words will not be enough, this I know is true,
The least I can offer, is the knowing that an apology is due.

Since motherhood, I've carried weight of guilt,
Awakened from my past, by present sharply built.

Memories of words serrated and cold,
Stubbornly snarling, emotions untold.

She mothered me, with devotion's embrace,
Our dance uncoordinated, two souls finding grace.

Now I know the labor, unlearning my own wrong,
To raise another, love's painful song.

A new set of eyes, at birth's sacred door,
I bear the guilt I've caused her before.

I could and should have given more, I rue,
If only I had known, what I now do.

Innocent mom, my dear Bambi so pure,
I weep for your soul, for all you endure.

I'll never match your strength, steadfast and true,
You toiled and toil, shielding me from what I never knew.

I should have been better, I deeply confess,
If only I had known, the depth of your selflessness.

A thousand times, I'm sorry for words that stung,
Spiteful daggers, from my heart they sprung.

Now I see your efforts, unwavering and grand,
Caring and selfless, deserving homage, I stand.

"Love is when he gives you a piece of your soul, that you never knew was missing."

Torquato Tasso

RUNNING FOR THE THRILL

There is something about the pace of London that throws a carpet underneath your soles and eloquently sweeps it from underneath you. As you try and regain your balance you cant help but notice that there is this excitement in the air that tickles your nose into a sneeze and can make your eyes water from the countless possibilities.

Fortune stands among you on a daily basis, showing itself to be reachable and so wonderfully tangible. The frivolity of London snaps and nips at your heels and nudges you along with the utmost confidence and care.

But home is home and it sings my name with a haunting harmony. It calls for me every so often and the memory lulls me to sleep. It aches of warm food on those white snowy evenings. It pours love deep and syrupy, constantly steady. Infectious is the knowing of where you're going and the pure knowledge in knowing at all!

Those familiar emotionally warm faces that smile at you and engulf you with "Oh how I've missed you","how good it is to see you again," "come sit here, and tell me all about it" are harpoons to my heart from a place now so far away.

My urge to experience, to explore, to leave was deafening. The noise had to be reconciled with. The door seems wide open and not just a jar any longer. My new life seems like a vacation from my old one and in contrast seems like a departure from normalcy.

And so, as I pushed myself onto the tube, practically hugging a stranger, I gripped my shawl around my neck to ward off the bellows of Old Man Winter. I realized I had found happiness and was finally at peace from the restlessness that had consumed me.

ASSERT

Infancy, quite literally, signifies the absence of spoken words. It is through the art of communication that we transcend this stage, for it imparts the ability to convey messages beyond mere infantile demands. Within the intricate tapestry of language lies an entire framework of meaning, capable of transforming a mere world into a cherished home, connecting us to the warmth of community, and eradicating the pervasive sense of isolation. Understanding and belonging within a community are integral to a truly fulfilling life. When we voice our thoughts and communicate our feelings, we shed the shackles of infancy and become participants in the realm of understanding.

However, to adopt a passive-aggressive stance, withholding our thoughts and feelings, is to regress to infantile standards and impose upon ourselves a self-inflicted punishment of submission. Language, a liberating gift bestowed upon us, holds immense power. If we find ourselves yearning to be understood, instead of succumbing to frustration and closing ourselves off, let us initiate open discussions and display restraint against the pull of infancy.

By embracing the freedom of language, we engage in expressionism that serves as a bridge, connecting us to our community, friends, and the vastness of the outside world.

In the amalgamation of language, communication, and freedom lies our liberation from the constraints of infancy. This profound union empowers us to transcend our limitations, allowing our voices to soar and our thoughts to resonate. It is through this transformative journey that we emancipate ourselves, finding solace in being truly understood and weaving unbreakable bonds within the vibrant tapestry of human existence.

FOREVER BOND

A true best friend is an operation that is conjoined.
It's one-self.
One truth.
An honest opinion with no blind spots.

EX NIHILO

Out of nothing, something can be born. From a void, a beauty emerges, stories may unfold and creation may take its form.

The virtue of stillness is not an empty space; rather, it is a profound sanctuary that carries significant weight, drawing you into the present with an irresistible allure. Within this sacred space of stillness lies the true masterpiece—the opportunity for intimate self-reflection. Through the lens of Taoism, we observe and allow the spirit to flow effortlessly. It is in the act of letting things be that we discover the depths of silence, where profound wisdom resides, while superficial chatter remains shallow.

In a world driven by constant motion, the skill of stillness is a challenging path to navigate. Society often associates flourishing with continuous action, disregarding the power of simply allowing life to flow. However, I have come to realize that in embracing the art of letting it flow, we actively engage with life, experiencing its richness and finding harmony within ourselves. Out of nothing, something can be born.

DEPOSITS

Build a life from the stars, sea, and sand.
Allow your spirit to dance with the rhythm of the tide.

Release your dreams to imprint like constellations.
Unveiled or revealed like stars against the darkness.

With searing hope, in skies of azure blue,
The world, my turtle doves, is all for you.

OLD LADY LOVE

The longing to understand the enigma of Old Lady Love has steadily grown within me. That profound awakening commenced when I began to fathom the intricacies of devotion.

Initially, Old Lady Love paid me no mind, intensifying my craving for her attention. I yearned to immerse myself in her wisdom, walking beside her to unlock the secrets of complete companionship.

When her gaze finally turned towards me, fear gripped my heart. Like a quivering leaf, she extended her veiny, blue hands for me to hold, but I recoiled, stumbling over my clumsy feet. Her hand seemed both menacing and unfamiliar.

Old Lady Love patiently waited until one day, without my knowledge, she gently transferred me into his care. My heart surrendered, and I accepted, as did he. No longer did I grasp onto her frail, sun-spotted hand, but I found solace in his embrace.

The cold nights dissipated, and a radiant rainbow emerged in the once eerie darkness. Its vibrant prism of colors shimmered, fractured, and danced, exuding a profound sense of pleasure and healing.
Little fissures of pleasure wounds, like delicate whispers or thunderclaps of love's fierce storm.

RELEASE

I cry at night
so you don't have to hear it
in my voice the next morning.

MOTHERLY HUES

Motherhood is like being given the ability to paint with colours I never knew existed.

DEATH

When we die, I pray for it to feel as though you're cradled in love's soft nap.

Like when you'd fall asleep as a child during a family party, only to be scooped up half-awake.

I hope that death is like being carried to bed while hearing laughter drifting in from the next room, with dreams gently draped.

HUNGRY SOUL

Feed your spirit,
Not the crowd.

HEARTACHE

A fractured heart, if fortune favours, becomes a part of life.

In due course the ache will invariably lessen to a minuscule grain of grit, a universe in itself.

Yet, amidst its midst, it's akin to being blinded from a furious fist full of sand.

"We are writers, my love. We don't cry. We bleed on paper."

Jeanette LeBlanc

Thank
You

our time has come
to a close
from start to end
a farewell rose.

the final act fades
curtain descends with grace
applause resounds
bows embrace.

Natasha Soares

www.ingramcontent.com/pod-product-compliance
Lightning Source LLC
Chambersburg PA
CBHW042129100526
44587CB00026B/4235